Winter Homes

Winter Homes

Cozy Living in Style

images
Publishing

Contents

Introduction

There is a simple pleasure in being inside during inclement weather. Something that perhaps speaks to our primal ancestry when we can feel secure and warm inside a dwelling, despite the frightful weather outdoors. There's something about the warmth of the beckoning interior lights set against a wintery evening or a stormy night that speaks about sanctuary from the elements, and promises warmth and security. A stylishly appointed, cozy interior in which to enjoy the warmth and comfort.

Architects design residences to take into account all sorts of conditions, but perhaps designing for the cold is of most importance when it comes to human comfort. Winter conditions can range from fog or sleet, rain that either pelts down or drizzles constantly, to light dustings of snow or more extreme blizzards. There is the intense cold that freezes eyelashes, with wind-chill factors that stagger the mind, but there is also the inescapable damp cold that seeps into your bones. And whatever the elements might have at their disposal, the home must remain warm and cozy, providing an elemental security against the might of nature as well as being a pleasant and cheerful place in which to live.

As technology continues to improve, residential architecture reaps the benefits. Insulation has improved greatly, and keeping a home toasty warm is much easier in the modern age. Thermal massing can provide heat gain that can be stored, resulting in less energy usage. Double- or triple-glazed windows ensure that there is no heat loss, despite the potential ferocity of tree-bending winds outside. Radiant floor heating and ERV (energy recovery ventilation) are becoming more common, and even home automation systems as used in Chalet Whymper (France). And, with the current challenge of residents bearing the brunt of climate change, there are the obvious benefits of keeping energy costs down. In the short term, there is the welcome lowering of energy bills, a wonderful saving for the wallet and house budget. Plus there is the warm glow of knowing you are helping the planet.

There are also health benefits, both physical and mental, to take into consideration. A house that has cold draughts throughout can impact negatively the resident's immune system, making them ill, as well as cold and miserable, stuck in a home that is not comfortable. Instead of a sanctuary, the residence becomes a place that must be endured. Anyone who has lived in an inadequately designed home will know the draining effects of trying to keep warm, of having to put the oven on for extra warmth, and being unable to sleep well at night despite numerous blankets. A home that has poor ventilation can result in mold, with its associated ill effects. An interior space that remains bright and cheerful can also help to keep the winter blues at bay. Adding a touch of yellow to a feature wall, for instance as seen in the Anker-Jordan Residence (United States), can add an extra bit of visual warmth, providing a cheery contrast to the gray outdoors. Wooden beams or flooring soften the interiors while bestowing a visual warmth as well. The addition of a fireplace grants a touch of coziness, as well as the chance to toast marshmallows indoors.

There are other intricacies involved in designing a winter home. The external cladding or elements must be able to withstand not only summer sunshine, but also the biting cold, and not deteriorate. Merri, with its aluminum shingles, will last a lifetime and not require any painting or maintenance. Locations with lots of snow will require a place to divest your outdoor garments so as to not traipse snow throughout the interior of the house, leaving them to dry in readiness for their next use. The home's structure must also be able to withstand strong winds and high snow loads. When designing Langlois-Lessard Residence (Canada), the architects positioned and angled the roof so it could withstand the fierce winds that blow in from the west. Heavy snow load is accounted for with a sloping roof, one with a smooth gradient as seen in Öjersjö Villa (Sweden), but also often with a steep, high-pitched gable, such as demonstrated by the Hatley Residence (Canada).

Consideration must also be given to where the snowmelt will go. Cabin Kvitfjell (Norway) ingeniously deals with the issue of snowmelt by raising the structure above the ground on stilts. Even something as simple as being able to go from inside the home to the garage without going outside is useful when there is snow on the ground for months at a time. A covered porch or walkway keeps areas free from snow, and safe to traverse, while a wooden lattice can help to prevent snow accumulating around the house.

With careful thought, it is possible to position a house or angle the windows such that it allows any available winter sun to penetrate the interior, providing welcome rays of light. Efjord Retreat (Norway), for instance, was positioned carefully in the terrain not only to accommodate impressive views, but also for solar orientation, allowing natural light to wash through the interior. Large and expansive floor-to-ceiling glazed windows are a common feature, such as seen in the Stormvillan residence (Finland), and maximize not only the view but allow the sunshine to bathe the interior spaces. A central patio or courtyard is another mechanism for delivering light into the inside of a home, as seen in Long House (United Kingdom), or even the introduction of skylights, as used in House of Many-Worlds (Norway).

Visually, a residence aglow with illumination throughout provides a pleasing contrast to the wintery moody exterior, a welcome lantern that beckons the inhabitant indoors, promising shelter and warmth. And there's a childlike wonder in being able to remain indoors in the warm but looking out to the wintery wonderland outside, or being able to enjoy a hot cup of tea while looking at the rain on a window. A successfully designed winter home is one that protects against the elements but also provides a stylish interior, with an abundance of coziness.

Anker-Jordan Residence

Ossipee Lake, NH, United States

Nestled on a wooded peninsula with views over the water, this modern but cozy holiday home provides warmth and security throughout all the seasons, but particularly during wintery weather, when the bone-chilling winds sweep up from the lake, or crisp icy frost sets in.

This ingenious design forms a modern cottage comprising two conjoined prisms, providing an elegant resolution to a wide range of desires and concerns as expressed in the original client brief. The client family wanted a place where three generations could gather together throughout the seasons to spend time, but they also stipulated that the construction be environmentally friendly with the ability to sit lightly within its spectacular surrounds.

The design needed to take into account the complexities of the site location, with sparse sunshine on the south side while the northern face is buffeted by cold winter winds. It also needed to allow for the ever-changing views of the lake, forests, and the White Mountains range.

Using a process of adaptive computational design, the architect developed an elemental prism that maximizes interior volume while affording a high passive environmental efficiency and minimum impact on the site. The folded roof simultaneously negotiates the southern exposure, the northern views, the management of snow precipitation, and the summer westerly winds. The interior of the prism is articulated as interconnected cells that provide increased social interaction.

The striking design not only provides shelter during the summer months (including overcast inclement days), but comes into its own during fall and winter, with the glow of lights providing a pleasing contrast to the gray skies and moody surroundings. The internal color scheme works well in all seasons, but the punches of yellow add an extra bit of visual warmth during the cooler months. The addition of a wood-fire gives the final touch of coziness, letting the residents enjoy the warmth of the muted contemporary interior design while gazing out onto the trees swaying in the cold wind.

Breac.House

Horn Head, Donegal, Ireland

Carefully positioned in the beautiful Donegal landscape, Breac.House is a stunning modern residence. A sensitive reworking of an existing building, the end result exceeded the expectations of the owners.

The owners had long been admirers of MacGabhann Architects, and in particular appreciated the firm's ability to deliver contemporary design solutions that were both visually arresting but also at one with the incredible Donegal landscape. So when the decision was made to convert an existing 1980s bungalow into a high-end bed-and-breakfast, there was only one firm they approached. The clients desired a genuine collaboration that would combine the many ideas which they had themselves developed with the design and execution expertise that MacGabhann could bring.

Both the owners and the designers shared a common wish to use the best quality local materials and tradespeople wherever possible.

The architects set about reconfiguring the design of the original building, organizing the kitchen, dining, and patio spaces to face the southwest, while the generously sized bedrooms face the southeast, with views over Sheephaven Bay and Derryveagh Mountains.

With its simple lines and muted tones, the revamped structure places an emphasis on the surrounding landscape. The long building, with its gently sloping roof, is reminiscent of Muckish Mountains in the distance, thus embedding the building into the landscape. The long, low exterior deliberately disappears into the heather-clad hillside. Constructed of stone, metal, and glass, the building is wrapped in wooden larch cladding. The wooden cladding has been treated with Shou Sugi Ban to protect it from the wet and damp elements. Inside, the interior space is light and bright, and exudes an air of serenity.

Breac.House celebrates Irish craftsmanship, with an emphasis on local materials and is a stunning and exciting design that is at once both contemporary and traditional.

Cabin Kvitfjell

Kvitfjell, Norway

Situated at one of the highest points within the Kvitfjell Ski Resort, where the topography drops dramatically providing uninterrupted views toward the southeast, this stunning ski cabin provides a welcome refuge in the snowy landscape.

Raised above the ground on stilts, the cabin is specifically designed
to rest on the ground in the lightest manner possible. This ingenious
solution also allows the residence to withstand the deep snows of winter,
as well as the dramatic snowmelt and runoff during spring.

The plan of the main cabin has a Y-shape that cantilevers out to frame
the remarkable views over the mountains from both the living area
and the master bedroom.

A courtyard is created by placing the two building volumes close to the site boundary. The façade toward the courtyard is clad with thin, vertical timber louvers with large panes of glass behind, giving the wall a veil-like quality, and adding to the sense of the "summer cabin in the winter landscape," as desired by the client. The louvers also protect the glass façade from snow, thereby maintaining a clear route of access all year. This outdoor area opens toward to the west, optimizing the evening sun and providing increased privacy from neighbors.

The living area, clad in light wood, has an expansive window through which the inhabitants can take in the stunning view down the slope, while basking in the warmth of the wood-fired heater. The glazing also allows the winter sunshine to penetrate into the home.

Casa Myhrer Hauge

Oslo, Norway

This house was designed not only to provide a cozy sanctuary during the northern winter, but to find a dialog between architecture and nature. The small stream on the site was revealed in its rippling glory, landscaped and returned to nature as a visual and influential element. This natural element provides a memorable experience as you enter the house via the bridge, accompanied by the sound of trickling water and, in summer time, the birds singing. Thus, the house itself is not taking anything away from nature, it is bringing nature back, and even emphasizing the encounter with nature.

The architectural aesthetics are based on a clear choice of materials, the wooden base and the raised plaster-volume creating the instrument to play with compositions. The simple and rather strict columns and bridges bear a resemblance to the wooden tree-trunks surrounding the site, simultaneously giving a modernistic, even functional association to the architectural history. The bridge continues inside the house, and makes an architectural clarification of the volumes and concept. The partly two-story living room has a playful and exciting spatial difference, providing access to both the television room upstairs and the roof terrace. This also gives the possibility to understand the architecture and concept of the house from different settings, angles, and elevations.

The kitchen and dining areas are integrated in the overall layout of the plan, becoming a distinct part of the living room, although defined by a lower ceiling.

The materials are simple, with a soothing color palette with natural materiality that, in spite of its modern denomination, responds and belongs to the nature surrounding it.

Chalet du Bois Flotté

La Malbaie, QC, Canada

Located on a sloping terrace overlooking Cap-à-l'Aigle and the Malbaie River, this home is reminiscent of the first homes built along St Lawrence Valley with their gabled roofs.

Two buildings join at right angles to create a design as rustic as it is refined. The steel of the roof (which extends in places to cover the walls) together with the cedar cladding of the gables (also used in parts of the side walls) create a striking combination.

The oxidation from contact with sea air will gradually give the cedar the silvery hue characteristic of seaside dwellings. The chalet's uniform shapes best frame the landscape, allowing access to the grounds via a terrace where the two buildings meet. The name means "Driftwood Chalet," with its colors reminiciscent of a piece of driftwood driven onto the coast by the winds and tides.

Large windows give occupants a view of the region, taking advantage of the opulent beauty of the landscape. The chalet can be described as humble and discreet, offering a haven of relaxation while managing to be cost-effective, with simple lines that do not compromise comfortable contemplation and enhancement of the view. The interior has a minimalist Scandinavian flavor, but the jewel in the design is the immense glass wall that covers the chalet's entire western face.

The clients wished for a new family space where they could relax among friends and family, and enjoy the unobstructed view of the river below, the changing skies and landscapes. They also wished for harmony with nature, so the architects came up with a limited footprint and overall compact layout and aimed to construct the residence in an ecologically friendly manner. The result is a home grounded on land while offering bespoke views of the river and valley, creating a true connection with the surrounding nature.

Chalet la Petite Soeur

Lac Ouareau, QC, Canada

On the vast Lac Ouareau sits a charming traditional house surrounded by birch trees, which was in great need of an extension for the use of the large family who owned it. In order to make sure everyone in the family can find a peaceful corner when spending time together, the architects created an addition that mirrors the original building's dimensions. The extension, with its modern clean lines, preserves and pays tribute to the historic house while reflecting the beauty of the landscape it inhabits.

The new space – a white prism standing on a concrete pedestal – appears like a refined version of the existing house. Through this contrasting effect, the extension maintains a connection to the original building and its location. The sheet metal roof and wood cladding resemble the smooth and shiny bark of birch trees growing on the site; the hues and textures also recall the whitewashed walls of countryside barns.

On the ground floor, an open-plan space and large windows allow spectacular views to the lake. Polished concrete floors and natural wood details are used with simplicity, emphasizing the materials' richness. Surrounded by black slatted wood, the central fireplace creates a relaxing ambience and an oasis of comfort in the vast living room. Built-in benches offer private spaces in common areas and cleverly include hidden storage. The living room and its gaming table encourage the children to make the space their own, providing playful and relaxing family time.

The transition from the old house to the new one takes place on a glass bridge. From the extension, an oak wood frame directs views toward the inside of the existing house, the frame's warm shade matching the old wood planks. The truncated shape of the bridge makes it wide enough to occupy: a welcomed pause in the landscape, floating over a garden. The bridge's axis aligns the kitchen of the existing building and the new living room.

Chalet Whymper

Chamonix-Mont-Blanc, France

At risk of being abandoned as an unfinished construction, Chalet Whymper
was taken on by the architect firm who could see the possibilities of the
site, and who went on to produce an impressive holiday home. This chalet
has location in spades, and is situated close to a protected wilderness,
and set against a stunning mountain backdrop, with a spectacular view
of three iconic French alpine peaks: the two Drus and Aiguille Verte.
No wonder the firm couldn't pass it by.

Featuring a winning combination of classic chalet design and modern sharp lines, the residence has generous windows, which provide ample daylight in the living areas, and impressive internal volumes of space, allowing for a luxuriously comfortable stay. Highlighting the views was uppermost on the minds of the designers, and accordingly one of the kitchen walls is simply a glass panel, with a breathtaking outlook onto Whymper Couloir. The lounge area boasts expansive windows, providing an almost 360-degree view. If this wasn't enough, the pool located in the basement features a window well framing the beautifully picturesque scenery.

The fireplace and low ceiling with embedded wooden beams in the lounge add to the sense of coziness. The mezzanine, suspended above the lounge, is an example of a solution implemented to fulfill one of the owner's desires, without compromising the view of the Aiguilles de Chamonix mountains. The chalet is equipped with the latest technology, including highly advanced home automation systems, integrated into the project from the very beginning, and ensuring energy efficient heating in the snowy conditions.

Outside, the blizzard may rage and the winds howl against double-glazed windows, but the inhabitants remain toasty warm inside, ensconced in contemporary luxurious surroundings within this well-built home.

Dogtrot

Jackson, WY, United States

When designing a new home in the wilds of Wyoming, consideration for heavy snowfall must be given. Situated in a quiet meadow with 360-degree views of the surrounding ranchlands, foothills, and Glory Peak, this residence successfully combines simplicity with interest.

The design references its agrarian surroundings and is based on the concept of a dogtrot barn, two separate but connected forms. The long rectangular residence is connected to a separate garage structure by a three-foot-thick roof. There, a large central cutout lightens the mass, creates a focal point, and causes a dynamic play of light upon the correspondingly scaled planter below it.

The roof of the main structure is asymmetrically gabled, and is able to withstand the high snow loads. This modern take on the barn lends energy and opens up the interiors toward the primary views. The large windows allow natural light to brighten the interior, even when the outside is blanketed with snow. Although the house is one gabled form, protected outdoor spaces are carved out of the main volume and extended on either end, where perforated siding adds texture and provides covered porches with privacy and protection from the elements.

Throughout, materiality is minimal. The exterior is clad in oxidized steel, the interiors expressed in steel, glass, and concrete. The only wood used is larch, warm, light and rustic in character. In places it wraps up the walls to the ceiling and continues outside. The home's central open space is bracketed by the kitchen and a cast-in-place concrete fireplace; bedrooms lie at either end, opening onto the protected terraces.

The modernist space was designed to be warm, inviting, and livable. Inspired by the owners' love of nature, artifacts, color, and collections, furnishings include modernist lighting (like the tumbleweed chandelier in the living room), whimsical objects, such as taxidermy specimens from the owners' collection, and injections of color, particularly the vibrant rug in the living room.

Drama is a constant factor — in the sense of space created by the width and span of the connector roof; in the entry, with its oversized pivoting door flanked by glass; in the way the interiors open up to the views; and in bold and whimsical interior details — creating the perfect venue for a dynamic couple's retirement years.

Efjord Retreat

Halvarøy, Norway

Efjord is in a branch off the Ofoten fjord, in northern Norway. The site is
positioned on an island called Halvarøy on a natural ledge in the terrain
overlooking the fjord to the west, two of Norway's most challenging climbing
peaks toward the south, and protected by a ridge in the terrain toward the east.
Needless to say, the views are superb in any direction.

The client desired a retreat that focused on the panoramic views of the site, but also transported them to a feeling of isolation and total privacy, away from hectic work days in the city. The conceptual layout opens and closes the building in different directions, where the eastern part of the cabin closes toward some neighboring buildings and opens toward a ridge and the close terrain on the other side. The opposite directions are sought at the front end of the cabin, opening up to the magnificent views toward the dramatic mountains and the fjord to the west.

The two volumes are slightly offset to provide for sheltered outdoor areas and views toward the fjord from the rear volume. Generously sized glazing allows the resident to partake in the stunning views without fear of venturing outside into the cold. A wood-fired heater adds an extra layer of warmth and coziness.

The cabin is placed at the same height as the existing terrain to allow the outdoor spaces to interact seamlessly with the natural landscape. The terrain itself provided a natural orientation and positioning of the building that allows the different functions to work in tune with the movement of the sun and the balance between privacy and views.

The exterior of the cabin consists of two materials: structural glazing and core pinewood. The wood is treated with iron sulfate to achieve an even patina. The interiors are clad in birch veneer, the floors in granite tiles, as per the stone outside. Both types of wood are typical for this region. The sauna interiors and the ceiling of the sauna and bathrooms are clad in aspen slats because of the hygroscopic properties of the wood.

Five Shadows

Teton Village, WY, United States

Lying on the fringes of a meadow on a prime site at the base of the Teton mountain range, Five Shadows belies the density of the surrounding area. Slightly elevated above its neighbors, the compound imparts a feeling of privacy, screens nearby buildings through structural orientation and strategic window placement, and takes in broad views across the valley to the Gros Ventre Range.

The project, reminiscent of a homesteader's settlement, was developed with a vision of five connected symmetrical agrarian forms with minimal overhangs – a compound of buildings organized to accommodate an extensive residential program. The primary mass hosts the public spaces, the peripheral volumes capitalize on privacy for bedrooms and a den. The three central

forms are linked by glassy connectors; they lie parallel to and offset from each other. The remaining two forms in turn help define a series of distinct and different outdoor experiences, including the auto court at the entry, a west-facing courtyard that embraces an aspen grove, and a south-facing pool terrace flanked by a detached poolhouse.

The exteriors are clad simply in stone, with subtle steel detailing. A similarly minimal palette of rift-sawn white oak and white plaster informs the interior spaces, creating an enhanced sense of spaciousness and a light, bright interior. The seeming simplicity of forms and materiality is the result of rigorous alignments and geometries, from the stone coursing on the exterior to the sequenced wood plank coursing of the interior. The layout of the multiple buildings lends an elegance to the flow, while the relationship between spaces fosters a sense of intimacy. The formal proportions, material consistency, and painstaking craftsmanship in Five Shadows were all deliberately considered to enhance privacy, serenity, and a profound connection to the outdoors.

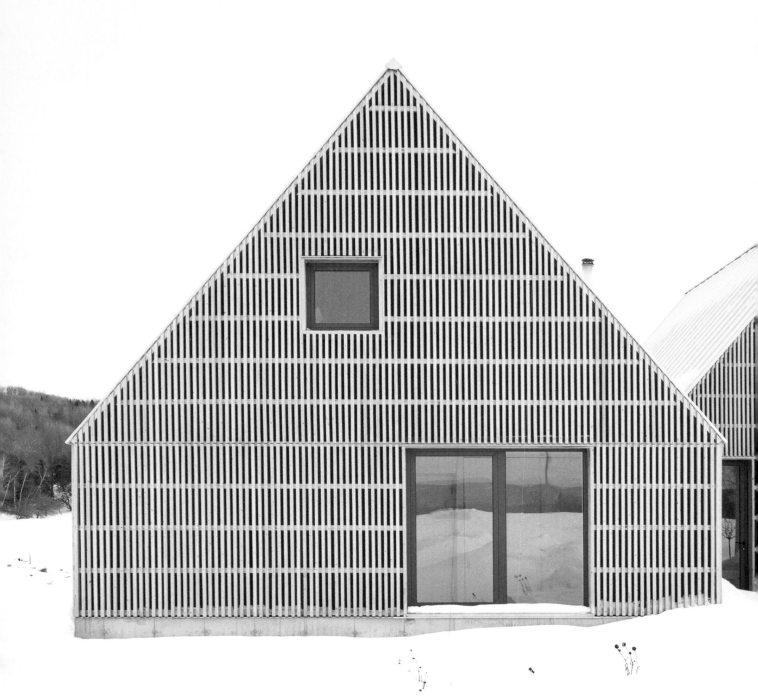

Hatley Residence

Hatley, QC, Canada

This residence gains its name from the nearby town of Hatley. Approaching the house from the nearby dirt road, one immediately recognizes the high-pitched gables typical of the area..

The roofline stands out above the rolling hills: three gables clustered together in an unusual way. The house is built on a natural plateau, providing a breathtaking panoramic view of the surrounding countryside and the mountains beyond. This landscape is defined by rolling hills, pastures, forest and mountains with farmhouses, barns and sheds scattered within this scenery. The house uses these elements from the original agricultural structures, reinterpreting them in a more abstract way and combining them with modern materials.

Three identically shaped volumes of varying sizes and orientation are connected side by side without ever intersecting. Together, they form an uncommon yet coherent ensemble. The shape of the house constantly changes as you move around it, while always remaining clear and intelligible. Three surrounding courtyards form a square around the house. The steep standing seam metal roof and deep timber lattice façade echo the nearby constructions.

The house is composed of three wings: the central communal wing, the master wing, and the guest wing. All three wings have double-height spaces. The two smaller wings also have more private wood-clad mezzanines above the bedrooms. Inside the house, large windows frame carefully selected views onto the agrarian landscape, while skylights in every double-height space fill the interiors with natural light throughout the day.

A few key structural elements define the house: the continuous horizontal concrete foundation, the deep timber lattice façade that wraps around the entire house, and the unified galvanized steel roof, all of which help link the volumes to one another. These structuring elements are meant to unify the architecture without simplifying it. The house is truly multi-layered. It is at once simple and complex, discreet and imposing, open and introverted, bare and luxurious.

House in Reilstad

Reilstad, Norway

Norway, known for its beautiful fjords, is home to spectacular views. Here, this holiday home is on the island of Finnøy, an island characterized by its typical Norwegian fjord landscape. But it is more than just a summerhouse, resting quietly and securely on its steep plot, looking toward the sea over rocky outcrops and visible bedrock. It also can function as a safe abode during inclement weather, allowing the residents to look out onto a wintery landscape in warmth and comfort.

Here the residents live on four levels, and move through an inner landscape that is connected to the exterior landscape on every level. In this way the house is organically adapted to the unique context. The roof slopes down with the terrain, in a sensitive approach to the landscape: using only natural materials and adapting the form to the steepness of the site.

The timber structure lies on a concrete slab, while cellulose fiber, used as insulation, keeps the home warm. Not only is there a sauna for use in both summer and winter, but a fireplace is placed between the two levels, adding an extra level of comfort. Each surface has its own depth and texture with its own spatial rhythm that enhances the adjacent outdoor nature: the ash-wood flooring with its marked grain, the fan-shaped staircase, the room furniture with an even ash finish and built-in shelving and niches, and the timber battens between the long roof-beams in the ceiling.

A floating roof covers the whole structure, only held up by the façades and ridge beam. From the entrance on the highest level one gets an overview of the whole house and down to the quay. The large roof creates a generous common space where everything is shared. From here there are views in every direction. All other rooms open on to this room. Some rooms appear as furniture as their internal ceilings do not connect to the floating roof. Within this array of spaces there are quiet spaces, intimate spaces, areas for working out or watching television. Or perhaps simply gazing out in awe at the silence of the wintery surroundings or a bank of rain moving in over the expanse of water.

House in Roschino

Roschino, Russia

The biting cold of a Russian winter is not to be underestimated. Located near Saint-Petersburg, this home was built for two artists, who wanted a comfortable residence for their family, and to be able to experience the beauty of nature. Nestled charmingly among the picturesque evergreen trees, you can immediately see how the soul of an artist would be quite at home here.

The site, just at the edge of the forest, has a bit of a slope, and is covered with conifer trees, adding a welcome touch of green during the long winter months. The existing trees directed the position and dimensions of the new building. The long narrow volume of the house is placed in such a way that it preserves all the flora and fauna of the site.

The house is divided into two parts: the main residence and an art studio, both separated by a transit porch. The residential part consists of an entrance area, a kitchen-living-dining area, two bedrooms for children and guests, and a master bedroom. The interior has clean lines and large open windows to feel close to nature. The dark floor provides a contrast to the white walls, almost drawing a line underneath the windows that bring nature right up to the house. The exterior of the house is faced with carbonized wooden planks, introducing the dark color into the whole house palette, and providing a stunning contrast to the dark green of the trees and the white of the winter snow.

Following the plot's slope, the floor level rises from the workshop to the bedrooms, while the roof level is set constant. The roof slopes to the south, so as to provide northern exposure to mezzanines in the bedrooms and the studio.

House in the Mountains

Bielsko-Biała, Poland

House in the Mountains is the modest, rural home for a five-person family. Situated next to Bielsko-Biała, on a long sloping site in the Beskid Śląski mountains, the home enjoys great views over the mountainous landscape and the nearby valley. The two-story building is integrated into the slope so that only the upper black volume is visible from the driveway. The structure is crowned with a traditional pitched roof covered with standing seam metal cladding.

The same material covers also the façade of this part of the building. This volume is additionally cut with a glass connector separating the main day zone from the bedroom. Windows of this level are designed in a way to provide southwestern lighting and scenic views of the surrounding mountain landscape. The lower floor, partially sunken into the hill, has been finished with architectural concrete slabs.

The lower level of the house includes an entrance area, garage with a technical room, and three bedrooms for children. This story on three sides is located below the existing ground level, and the fourth external wall opens to the garden with a view of the picturesque landscape of the Silesian Beskids.

The upper level consists of a living area with a master bedroom complete with its own bathroom and wardrobe. The day zone is centered around a wide kitchen island and a recreation area with a fireplace. Simple floor plans, high ceilings, and huge fixed windows framing mountainous views work together to enhance the sense of space of this house.

House of Many-Worlds

Oslo, Norway

With typical Scandinavian flair, this design is modest in nature, yet manages to pack a lot into its space, all with an elegant yet understated touch.

The main focal point of the interior is the open, double-height area in the center, where a large family table is positioned. Expansive windows provide a view to the nearby trees, and also enables the family to watch any visiting birds or frolicking squirrels.

The table allows ample space for family members to gather around it, occupied with different activities but in the same social situation. The windows and the skylights provide an abundance of natural daylight, even in the short winter days. Green interior plants and a warm suspended ceiling light add further to the cozy appeal.

The interior design is a contrast between black and white pigmented beech veneer, which gives the home a warm and light feel, and ties in well with its uncluttered design. The window seat offers an ideal spot to curl up and watch the antics of the animals and birds outside in the trees.

The loft forms the most intimate zone of the apartment. Protected by half-transparent perforated steel panels on either side, one can see the goings-on downstairs, or watch the snow pile up against the window, safe and snug inside, with the close proximity of the roof providing a sense of comfort and intimacy.

The overall effect is of a crisp, modern living space that employs the most up-to-date technologies to ensure warmth and natural light, while providing a secure place to observe the cold winter landscape outside.

House on the Slope

Baltic Riviera, Russia

Located on the coast with a breathtaking view over the Gulf of Finland, this project successfully achieves its objective to organically fit into the existing landscape, and preserve the existing trees and the huge stone boulder, which perched somewhat inconveniently in the middle of the site. The architect elected to make the incongruous rock a hero of the final design, with a small rock sculpture echo inside, with pleasing results.

The house comprises two volumes: the main residential volume and an additional guest house. The main residence is located high on the slope, while the guest house is embedded into the lower stepped relief, with the aim for both buildings to dissolve as much as possible into the landscape. The main house incorporates a retaining wall for the upper terrace while the guest house (with sauna) has a roof terrace incorporated into its design.

Both parts of the complex have panoramic glazing in the main rooms, allowing unrestricted views over the water. The warmth of the larch cladding adds a welcome touch of color when the landscape is coated with a heavy blanket of snow. The natural wood is continued inside the structure, with floorboards and cladding on the walls and ceilings. The color scheme is a muted icy gray, punctuated by the warmth of the natural wood features. Wooden shelves in the main living room continue the black of the window frames in the form of shelves, which contrast against the lighter wood backing.

A simple unadorned fireplace provides extra comfort during the northern winter, enhancing the feeling of warmth and adding to the sense of security and well-being, particularly when looking out at the huge snow drifts outside.

House with Gable

Rossleithen, Austria

Located on a slope just on the edge of a small settlement with superb views
over the alpine region of Pyhrn-Priel in Upper Austria, this house was designed
for a young family who wished to create a home that harmoniously matched
the surroundings, and brought the outdoors inside. The clients specifically
envisioned a calm, clear architecture comprising wood, concrete, and glass.
The result is this beautiful solid timber house, which succeeds in being
both simple and complex.

The simplicity is derived from the clear structure and proportion of the base, ground floor, and roof. The complexity comes from the spatial variety contained within.

At the high part of the slope the ground floor is located half a meter below terrain level, which creates a living space embedded by grassland. Down the slope, the kitchen and living room area is given enough space to unfold up to the ridge. The height picks up the topographic properties in an ideal manner and the slightly elevated position guarantees an excellent view of the mountains.

The family wanted an ecological focus in the design, and thus the land usage is designed to be modest as is the overall volume of the building. The compact size of the home forms a direct contrast to its larger neighbors. Cellulose fiber is used as insulation, to keep the interior warm. A minimalistic range of materials and forms has resulted in a maximum quality and comfort being achieved.

The interior is light and open, and flush with the warmth of pine wood cladding. The effect is spacious, enhanced by the generous white ceiling that forms a protective covering over the open space. Large glazed windows form a connection with the landscape outside, and can be slid open during warmer months. But in the winter when the snow lays outside in huge drifts, the windows offer a peak outside to the chilly landscape, while the family remains safe and secure in their home.

Langlois-Lessard Residence

Léry, QC, Canada

Sleek, crisp, and contemporary, this home is a response to the questions
raised when the architects visited the site on the shores of Lac Saint Louis.
The reflections included how to integrate architecturally with an exceptional
natural site and how to define the spatiality of the house, its volume and its
fabric in response to the site itself.

To preserve the pristine beauty of the site and its many mature trees, a compact footprint was adopted by the architects. Oriented toward impressive views and sunsets, the residence is sited near the water, creating the impression from within that the interior spaces are unfolding onto the lake.

Both the exceptional quality of the landscape and solar orientation of the site guided the general planning of living spaces on both floors, allowing natural light to penetrate into the interior. An open fireplace sits on the axis of the main entrance, at the heart of the volume, while service blocks detached from the exterior walls flank its sides, creating subtle sculptural volumes. Each floor is characterized by a remarkable spatial openness, yet the two are only connected through a very narrow and minimalist staircase. Inversely, on the second floor, the bedrooms enjoy interesting angular ceilings that generate a whimsical play of light and shadow. The volume of the house follows from two principles: to offer intimacy to the owners and to react to the strong winds that originate in the west. The roof has been shifted and angled in response to the surrounding natural environment. Glazed windows offer a further protection against the elements.

The elaborate integration of natural textures comes from an acute observation of the surroundings. Roughly shaped natural limestone, hemlock-textured concrete, and wood siding all work together to integrate the house to the natural tones of the site. Inside, the polished concrete floor and concrete fireplace dominate the material palette while the furniture softens and adds to the tone-on-tone effect. The neutral palette allows the place for the surrounding landscape, and its shifting seasonal experience to penetrate within.

Long House

Cirencester, United Kingdom

Winters in Britain are a varied beast, ranging from snow to sleet to cold winds. In the south, winters tend to be characterized by an unrelenting damp cold, which settles into your bones. This new home in the Cotswolds, however, keeps its inhabitants warm through the winter months while the brown hedgerows and bare trees outside bear witness to the cold.

The design reinterprets the rural vernacular and uses interlocking barn
forms and a palette of local materials. The front barn has been built in
drystone wall by a local craftsman, chosen not only for its local relevance
but for its inherent qualities of mass and muscularity. This traditional
stonework is echoed in the surrounding stone wall around the site. The
stone façade is monolithic, with fewer openings to produce a heavier, solid
volume at the front. As a counterpoint, the taller barn at the back is clad in
a lighter-weight natural larch that has been charred to a deep leathery black
at each window recess. This charring has then been brushed away to gently
blend it back into the natural larch – creating an ombré effect, which
emphasizes the rhythmic push and pull of the window indentations.

Inside, the key living spaces fan out around an internal patio, which acts as a focal point for the home. Clad in glazed ceramic tiles, the patio is a moment where both nature and light are introduced. The rays of sunshine provide a welcoming and warming influence on the interior. The interior design in the living room is a soothing combination of warm wood floors, with gray walls providing a contrast to the white ceilings. Elsewhere, a palette of white and light gray is used.

The construction meets passive house principles, and includes an insulated concrete formwork system creating a thermal envelope, limited openings on the south-facing façade, triple-glazed window units, and an energy heat recovery ventilation system to maintain air quality year-round.

The material choices anticipate a slow process of weathering and aging that will further embed the new home into its rural setting, and pay homage to the traditional buildings of the Cotswolds.

Malangen

Tromsø, Norway

This striking and angular modern house sits on the Malangen peninsula in Norway, and was designed for a family with small children, who also wanted to be able to invite friends to stay. From the first sight, the home's unusual angles and layout deliver a sense of intrigue. The location is picture-postcard perfect and the design contains surprises throughout.

Entry is through a beautiful door that virtually glows with light. Inside, a warm space awaits, with crisp modern tones and with the focus a delightful warm open fireplace, set in an understated dark chimney piece. The conceptual layout consists of several individual volumes, connected via in-between spaces and a central winter garden. This organization provides both privacy and room for several activities at the same time. It also reduces energy needed for heating in the cold climate, as various rooms and activities will require different temperatures.

The central winter garden, with fireplace and outdoor kitchen, functions as the entrance to the building. From here the retreat opens up to the natural clearing in the forest and from here you enter into either the main building or the annexe.

Each group of rooms are done as separate volumes to achieve an additional layer of privacy, but also to enhance the room's contact to the clearing in the forest and the contact to the outdoors in the transition spaces in between. There's even a small area set apart to offer a quiet place to relax, or play, or simply soak up the view.

A few steps lead down to the open-space kitchen and living room set low in the terrain and overlooking the fjord and the afternoon sun to the west. The view from the large window in the living room is simply stunning, in any season. A concrete wall houses a second fireplace, while a large sliding glass door opens the room to the outdoors in warmer weather. True to Scandinavian custom, there's also a sauna with one wall entirely glazed for basking in the warmth while looking at the snowdrifts outside.

All interiors are custom designed to complete a holistic structure and reference the function and activity to each designated space or room, whether outdoors or indoors. Choice of materials and detailing are carefully done to create clear definitions of integration or contrast, and reflect the spaces, individual relation to the outdoors or connecting rooms. The majority of the interior furnishing and furniture are all custom designed; Nordic style provides stylish comfort and warmth during winter.

Merri

Princeton, MA, United States

Tucked away in the woodland of Massachusetts, this home shimmers in
the sun, and provides a shining example of how a design can explore an
alternative definition of luxury, one that is attained through an honest
response to the site's context. In this case, the architect converted the
site's constraints into opportunity by connecting two identical barns,
one rotated to best fit the site. The result is an energy-efficient
two-barn composition inserted into the slope.

The façade orientations capture site-specific views and ample cross ventilation, simultaneously providing protection from the fierce northern winter. The footprint saves trees and protects existing wetland resources. The house is super insulated with radiant floor heating throughout, ERV (energy recovery ventilation) installed, supplemented with two wood stoves. After the first winter, the house proved itself to be cozy and comfortable during blistery cold days, and with a huge reduction in energy costs. With abundant cross ventilation, artificial air conditioning in summertime is not necessary.

Mill-finished aluminum shingles provide a sense of order to the exterior of this architecture. From a distance, Merri appears as a box with a familiar scale and form that blends in with the surroundings. On a closer approach, one starts to recognize the architectural discourse. Standing next to it, one understands the interlocking details and the beautifully articulated mechanism behind the complex expression. The house becomes one with the landscape, reflecting continuous gradation of surrounding colors, adding a sophisticated poetry to a simple life in the woods. These aluminum shingles are 90 percent recycled/recyclable, warrantied for a lifetime. Aluminum's physical property to reflect light is another significant contributing factor toward energy efficiency. Last but not least, this building is maintenance free. The aluminum retains its sheen, and does not require painting.

The process was a true collaboration between the architect and their client, both of whom were romantic, pragmatic, open-minded, and had a mutual determination to create a house by thinking "big" and acting "humble."

Mountain House

Manigod, France

Designing a new home in a strictly controlled heritage Alpine valley allows for very little freedom of architectural expression, with stringent guidelines in place to protect the existing vernacular tone. But through a careful analysis of the local historical buildings and what their forms accomplished functionally, the designers were able to create something entirely new, yet recognizably true to the history of the region.

In the context of a mountain house in the Alps, the way a building touches the ground was historically related to stables, woodshop, and storage. The design ensured that domesticity was expressed with subtlety and that some of the historical functionally was incorporated, conveying a continuation of the traditional building style.

The base of the house is made out of cast-in-place concrete with formwork using the same wood as above-floor cladding. The floors are then simply stacked above the base, each time projecting out further than the floor beneath so as to provide a greater protection similar to what greater roof overhangs provided in traditional buildings. Because the sides are no longer used for any specific functions there is no roof overhang on the sides. The first floor transitions between the more abstract concrete base and the top floor, which acknowledges directly the context with its pitched roof and large openings out to the valley.

Similarly the sequence of interior spaces starts off dark and compressed. Progressing up through the building, more light comes in and gradually more views are allowed out. Ceiling heights are gradually increased to reach their high point in the living area where a cross-shaped beam and column act as a reminder of the great snow loads the building needs to support. The end result stands as an example of how architecture can, and should, convey past knowledge into the present and protect it for the future.

Not only does the resulting home provide warmth and a secure abode in winter, but the careful design and use of materials gives a gracious nod to the previous architectural styles. This home is secure against the elements, and with a beautiful interior, decked out with light-colored wood, where natural light is able to pour through the upstairs windows.

Öjersjö Villaj

Öjersjö, Sweden

This contemporary but modest dwelling overlooks the lake Stora Kåsjön, while its sleek black exterior forms a direct contrast to the banks of snow in winter. Situated on a hill with neighbors on each side, the house consists of a number of displaced volumes. The aim therefore was to fit program and volume into the complex without compromising the lake view, but also to successfully tackle privacy issues relating to the site. Designed to be closed toward the street and open toward the view in the west, the home provides a warm interior during the Swedish winter.

The home is built with a wooden construction going from one floor in the north end of the building to two in the south. The straight tilted roof draws a contour both in alignment with and extruding from the house. The exterior is boarded with black calcimine color. The dark exterior is put in contrast to the solid wood interior.

The tilted roof structure also creates a sculpted interior with different heights and levels. The roof has a smooth gradient, perfect for dealing with large snow loads, leading from the ground floor of the garage toward the main point at the back of the house. The house benefits from extra space as the roof rises upward, ending with more than two floors at the highest point of the house.

The windows are designed with deep niches, perfect for sitting upon, and along with the rest of the interior are clad with wooden panels. The pine wood, sourced from northern Sweden, is treated in non-tinted hardwax for a natural raw look, and covers the walls, floor, and even the ceiling. The large windows, with their black frames, offer a beautiful aspect onto the surrounds and views toward the lake.

The interior is light and bright, providing an inviting space within. The contrast of the black external wood with the light pine cladding inside is classically appealing. The interior is sparsely furnished in an understated Nordic fashion. A large heater provides a focal point in the living area, and adds extra warmth. Large sliding glass doors give access to an outdoor terrace for when the winter finally moves on, and summer returns.

Pond Lily

Upstate New York, United States

Pond Lily is a striking modern lodge strategically sited on private lakefront property in upstate New York. The house is revealed as the scenic approach passes beneath magnificent willow trees alongside the spectacular lake.

The forms of the exterior integrate design elements indigenous to the pastoral countryside, such as stone and wood, as well as expanses of windows to capture views of the magnificent property, while the minimalist interiors create a quiet retreat and gallery-like space for the client's contemporary art collection.

The interior includes double-height cathedral-like spaces with grand scissor trusses, and boasts floor-to-ceiling glazing to celebrate its lakefront setting. The internal color palette is a soft white coupled with gray stone, a color repeated with some of the furniture. Upstairs features a warm wood floor while the downstairs living room is kept warm with a minimalist gray carpet. A landing with a glazed façade offers a view down to the stylishly appointed living area.

Sited to highlight views of the lake, the home is designed to appear connected to the lake and still feel integrated into the gradually sloped site. Originally envisioned as a more traditional lodge by the client, the home as designed by the architecture firm evolved into a more modern minimalist interpretation.

Locally sourced stone evokes a solid foundation that complements the modern yet durable natural wood cladding and gabled rooflines with accents of standing seam metal roofing, necessary to withstand the harsh winter weather in upstate New York.

Residence Maribou

Saint-Sauveur, QC, Canada

Originally built in the 1960s, the house featured the traits of that period's Scandinavian architecture, and followed the importance of functionality and materiality, which would be the keys to design. This "organic" architecture was brought to the forefront in this major transformation.

Although this house had several insulation and structural problems, its great singularity motivated the owners to invest in its renovation for their retirement project, instead of in a total demolition. The objective thus was to conserve its original character, while modernizing several of its aspects to improve the program's functionality. And staying warm during the freezing Canadian winter was, of course, a priority.

Apart from the restoration of the envelope and several interior elements, the main challenge was to review access to the residence in order to reduce the number of steps to climb from the parking. The main entrance, previously located on the second floor, was therefore relocated to the first floor, forcing a complete reorganization of traffic and the program.

For the interior, the strong elements represented by the big stone wall and the singular railing were conserved in their entirety and restored to context in a more contemporary composition. The new volumetry, freeing more space in the master bedroom, allows the addition of new fenestration opening on the landscape. On the main floor, new openings were made to finally give a view of the rocky landscape from the kitchen.

The residence, which previously had a "back room" exclusively orientated to the distant view, now offers a multitude of framings of different landscape scales. And answers the clients' need to have a warm and secure abode for their retirement, a haven against the cold winds and snow of winter.

Rundherum

Linz, Austria

Perfectly positioned with views of the surrounding trees and hills, this delightful home offers clean lines and a warm interior.

At first glance, the building resembles a square bungalow, with generous windows. An intensive redevelopment saw the inner structure of the original residence preserved, repurposed to serve as the core of the new building. The overall floor space was nearly doubled in size with the new additions. The new outer walls of wood and glass set the rhythm of the redesign.

The two architectural layers remain present and clearly recognizable: the internal white walls are original while the extension comprises glass and fir wood, with its glowing warm color. The untreated wooden construction, black windows, and the dark varnished maritime pine all work in unison to create a clearly structured façade with an unpretentious appearance as a pavilion in the landscape. The original saddle roof was replaced with a flatter version, tying together the minimalistic look of the walls. The roof is still able to cope with large snow loads.

Given the cold winters, the house has solid wooden floors throughout, with glazed windows, providing an internal volume that remains well-insulated. A solar system and an air-heating pump were added to keep energy use sustainable. Through the demolition of some of the internal walls, an open-plan living space has been created. The interior space is now light and bright, providing a stylishly warm abode, perfect for looking out of the large windows onto the snowbanks and snow-laden evergreens outside.

Stormvillan

Hanko, Finland

This stylish villa is located at the heart of the historic villa district of Hanko, a former popular spa resort for Russian nobility in the late nineteenth century while Finland was still a Grand Duchy under Russia. The endless meandering beaches are lined by leaning pine forests and grand wooden seaside villas. And while the spa may have fallen out of favor, the area still draws people wanting to relax in the natural surroundings, and enjoy the moody atmospheric conditions when the weather turns inclement.

The main floor opens out in three directions. The living room boasts a long view out to sea, the lounge faces west, giving access to glorious sunsets across the dining terrace, and the master bedroom takes in the junipers and wind-blown pinetrees of the cliff it stands on. Stormvillan is well-named, as the region encounters more than its fair share of storms. But, perched on its rocky base, this home will stand strong against the elements.

The ground floor cuts into the rock and the villa is entered at beach level. Visitors are guided through a narrow hallway with a glazed wall facing the revealed bedrock. At the very end of the ground floor is a room with two walls of bare bedrock, the wine cellar. A carpet-clad staircase leads up to the main floor. Designed as a home for an elderly couple, the villa also has an elevator and fully accessible bathrooms to make life comfortable. The main floor is about light, views, and flowing space. There is no room for brooding atmosphere here with its palette of white and light wood, casting a strong contrast to the outside gray or the solemnity of dusk. Its angles are designed to fit the natural shape of the rock as well as the fantastic views out to the sea.

The villa is clad in spruce panel, painted with traditional linseed oil paint as are the surrounding nineteenth-century villas. The roof of the ground-floor level serves as a wooden terrace with a section of green roof. The zinc roof blends into the coastal hues of the sky, and changes shades with the variable weather.

Stormvillan is a masterpiece in understated Scandinavian style, and provides warmth for its residents while its interior lights shine brightly during the dark days of winter.

Valley View

Whistler, BC, Canada

Crisp clear blue skies in wintertime are something to be treasured during the long Canadian winters. Contrasting beautifully against the snowy landscape and the determined foliage of the evergreens, it all combines to conjure up peacefulness and tranquility. And, above all, quietness.

No timid hiding behind a rustic and enclosed log cabin here though, as this house luxuriates in its surrounds, and confidently presents floor-to-ceiling glass windows on various fronts, to soak up the natural landscape outside.

Secure in the robust glazing and heating, the residents can elegantly lounge in the open-plan living room, beset on three sides with large panes of glass that serve to bring the external nature closer. The interior is clad with warm wooden panels, offering a touch of color in the white landscape. The fireplaces are constructed using large white granite, the rough-cut stones bestowing a human-scale texture.

Of course this isn't just a house for a winter landscape but, as the large outside porch and terrace suggest, Valley View awakens from its virtual hibernation during the warmer summer months, and throws open its doors and windows. But until that long-awaited day, this home provides the coziest and stylish mountain getaway this side of the prairies.

Vanella House

Corsica, France

Overlooking three major summits in the heart of Corsica, this guesthouse was designed to be part of the natural landscape, and to be able to withstand both the searing sun in summer and the biting cold of winter.

Constructed of granite and schist, the residence frames the main components of the landscape, a bit like an inhabited retaining wall. The design scheme deliberately evokes the retaining wall in front, with its flat roof echoing the shape of the wall.

The project plays with time through the use of its materials: the designers sought to tell a story through the mix of elements, such as concrete and stone, and also to serve as a reminder of traditional building methods in the past. Concrete is used in its truest way forming posts and lintels. Stone is used to fill the empty spaces of the structure. Inside, the lime plasters integrate and hide the technical elements.

The structure is illuminated by the western light, adding a warm glow to the stonework. The openings in the wall are designed to allow the natural light to penetrate inside, in a controlled and measured way. Large floor-to-ceiling windows offer unapparelled views out onto the landscape. The interior design reflects the color scheme of the stone, with the lime plaster providing a calm atmosphere, and the understated wooden furniture enhances this overall effect. The use of wood for the window and door frames adds a touch of warmth to contrast against the polished concrete.

Majestic chestnut trees dot the site, providing a dazzling focus point throughout the seasons, and revealing their stark silhouettes during the winter months.

Vermont Cabin

Stowe, VT, United States

What might seem at first glance to be a simple compact cabin is actually an efficient design that harbors a minimalist interior, nestled in the forest of Vermont, and providing a welcome refuge during the winter months.

Emerging from its hillside site, and rising into the white pines and maples that surround it, this structure was intended to bring the client's family members together, and reflect the traditional straightforward Vermont cabins from their childhoods. It was also the intention to bring the family closer to the wondrous nature that pervades the area, and as such the design took inspiration from its surrounds, resulting in an intimate gathering place among the trees. The cabin's modest footprint is an efficient and economical framework for the family to experience the heavily wooded landscape.

The cabin, with its elemental material palette of steel, wood, and concrete, is composed of three levels: the lowest portion nestles into the site and contains a garage that doubles as a game room, as well as a single bedroom and powder room; the middle portion consists of the main entry, two small bedrooms and a bathroom; and the top level is one large living area. Locating the main living spaces on the upper level maximizes views of the Green Mountains range to the west and the Worcester Range to the east. A single continuous stair of steel and maple hardwood connects all three levels.

Inside and out, materials are left in their raw states, with weathering steel external siding and exposed timber ceilings. The site's continuous slope and an external steel stair allow for dual entries on the lower and middle levels. Throughout, poured- and cast-concrete elements in the kitchen and bathrooms continue the cabin's emphasis on straightforward, simple materials, with radiant heat incorporated in the concrete floors of the main living area, keeping the residents toasty warm during the northern winter, while a wood fireplace adds that final touch of coziness. Exterior walls consist of concrete and weathering steel, along with large stretches of glass that deliver sweeping views of the landscape.

This is an intentionally straightforward and economical cabin where the family can come together and take part in the adventure of engaging with the natural landscape just outside.

Project Credits

Anker-Jordan Residence 12–19

Scalar Architecture
scalararchitecture.com

> **Location** Ossipee Lake, NH, United States
> **Completed** 2017
> **Photography** ImagenSubliminal
> (Miguel de Guzman & Rocio Romero)

Breac.House 20–27

MacGabhann Architects
macgabhannarchitects.ie

> **Location** Horn Head, Donegal, Ireland
> **Completed** 2017
> **Photography** Mike O'Toole, Paul McGuckin,
> Al Higgins

Cabin Kvitfjell 28–35

Lundhagem
lundhagem.no

> **Location** Kvitfjell, Norway
> **Completed** 2016
> **Photography** Marc Goodwin, Sam Hughes

Casa Myhrer Hauge 36–43

Gudmundur Jonsson Arkitektkontor
gudmundurjonsson.com

> **Location** Oslo, Norway
> **Completed** 2018
> **Photography** Jiri Havran

Chalet du Bois Flotté 44–51

atelier Boom-Town
boom-town.ca

> **Location** La Malbaie, QC, Canada
> **Completed** 2018
> **Photography** Maxime Brouillet

Chalet la Petite Soeur 52–59

ACDF Architecture
acdf.ca

> **Location** Lac Ouareau, QC, Canada
> **Completed** 2018
> **Photography** Adrien Williams

Chalet Whymper 60–67

Chevallier Architectes
chevallier-architects.fr

> **Location** Chamonix-Mont-Blanc, France
> **Completed** 2016
> **Photography** Solene Renault

Dogtrot 68–75

CLB Architects
clbarchitects.com

> **Location** Jackson, WY, United States
> **Completed** 2018
> **Photography** Matthew Millman

Efjord Retreat 76–83

Snorre Stinessen Architecture
snorrestinessen.com

> **Location** Halvaróy, Norway
> **Completed** 2017
> **Photography** Steve King

Five Shadows 84–91

CLB Architects
clbarchitects.com

> **Location** Teton Village, WY, United States
> **Completed** 2019
> **Photography** Matthew Millman

Published in Australia in 2021 by
The Images Publishing Group Pty Ltd
ABN 89 059 734 431

Offices

Melbourne
6 Bastow Place
Mulgrave, Victoria 3170
Australia
Tel: +61 3 9561 5544

New York
6 West 18th Street 4B
New York, NY 10011
United States
Tel: +1 212 645 1111

Shanghai
6F, Building C, 838 Guangji Road
Hongkou District, Shanghai 200434
China
Tel: +86 021 31260822

books@imagespublishing.com
www.imagespublishing.com

Copyright © The Images Publishing Group Pty Ltd 2021
The Images Publishing Group Reference Number: 1551

All photography is attributed in the Project Credits on pages 252–55, unless otherwise noted.
Pages 2–3: Matthew Millman (CLB Architects, Five Shadows); pages 6–7: Steve King (Snorre
Stinessen Architecture, Efjord Retreat); page 10: Matthew Millman (CLB Architects,
Five Shadows); page 254: Sindre Ellingsen (Helen & Hard, House in Reilstad)

 A catalogue record for this
book is available from the
NATIONAL LIBRARY OF AUSTRALIA National Library of Australia

Title: Winter Homes: Cozy Living in Style
Author: Jeanette Wall [Introduction]
ISBN: 9781864708660

Printed on 140gsm Maxi Offset paper at Graphius nv, in Belgium

IMAGES has included on its website a page for special notices in relation to this and its other
publications. Please visit www.imagespublishing.com

Every effort has been made to trace the original source of copyright material contained in
this book. The publishers would be pleased to hear from copyright holders to rectify any
errors or omissions.

The information and illustrations in this publication have been prepared and supplied
by the contributors. While all reasonable efforts have been made to ensure accuracy, the
publishers do not, under any circumstances, accept responsibility for errors, omissions and
representations, express or implied.